D0948259

Discard

SUPERSTARS OF FILM

mel gibson

Jon E. Lewis

CHELSEA HOUSE PUBLISHERS
Philadelphia

First published in traditional hardback edition
© 1998 by Chelsea House Publishers.
Printed in Hong Kong
Copyright © Parragon Book Service Ltd 1995
Unit 13–17, Avonbridge Trading Estate, Atlantic Road
Avonmouth, Bristol, England BS11 9QD

Library of Congress Cataloging-in-Publication Data
Noble, Sandy.
    Mel Gibson / by Sandy Noble.
       p.cm. — (Superstars of film)
    Originally published: London: Parragon Books, 1996.
    Filmography: p.
    Includes index.
    Summary: Presents the life and career of the Australian-
raised, American-born actor and film director.
    ISBN 0-7910-4643-5 (hardcover)
    1. Gibson, Mel—Juvenile literature.   2. Motion picture actors
and actresses—Australia—Biography—Juvenile literature.
[1. Actors and actresses.] I.Title.   II. Series.
PN3018.G5N63   1997
791.43'028'092—dc21
   [B]   97-26960
                                            CIP
                                             AC

CONTENTS

Mel Gibson

BEGINNINGS

On January 3, 1956, one of the least starlike of modern stars came into this world, in the small town of Peekskill in upper New York state. Unlike many other stars, he resents intrusions into his privacy, and he has resisted attempts to write official biographies. He views making movies as a job, and does not see what relevance his personal life has to those interested in his performances.

Mel Columbcille Gerard Gibson was the sixth of ten children born to Hutton and Anne Gibson. His parents were devout Catholics, of solid Irish stock. Mel's father had an extremely strong influence on how the family was brought up; Hutton's own father had been very religious and had passed this on to his son. As a young man, Hutton decided to enter the priesthood and attended a seminary, the Society of the Divine Word, in Chicago. However, he disliked the attempts of the Roman Catholic Church to make its liturgy more modern and he decided to quit. He joined the army and served in the Pacific in World War II. His experiences there made him determined that no children of his should ever serve in the military. He also visited Australia (his mother's native country), since it was a staging post for American GIs.

After leaving the army, Hutton took a job with the New

York Central Railroad to provide the means for a family that was expanding rapidly. New York City seemed an unsuitable place to raise a family so the Gibsons moved upstate, first to Croton-on-Hudson and then to a slightly larger home at Verplanck Point, also on the Hudson. This was to be Mel's first home.

Life in the Gibson household was run on severely moral grounds. Hutton's view of the world seems to have been quite fixed. With little money to go around, the family was left to entertain itself using its own resources, though the children found plenty to amuse them in the countryside. From an early age, Mel was an entertainer, using his charm and sense of humor to bend the rules.

Hutton dreamed of bringing up his family in an idyllic environment and he had originally hoped to be able to farm as well as hold down his railroad job. In 1961 the family moved to a farmhouse in Mount Vision, but unfortunately that location—two hundred miles north of New York— meant that, since Anne Gibson could not drive, the family spent all week in complete isolation while Hutton was away at work. Hutton was unable to find a suitably strict Catholic school, so the children went to a nondenominational school. Life was hard for the Gibsons, made significantly worse in 1964 when Hutton had a serious accident in the railyards and lost his job. The family had to move to a cheaper rented accommodation, and Mel's elder siblings, who were now young adults, took jobs to help out. Three years of fighting the railroad to gain compensation now began.

Hutton became increasingly despairing of life in the United States. In his eyes the sixties were a period of rapid moral decline—free love, psychedelic drugs, rock music at one end of the scale, and at the other extreme, escalation of the war in Vietnam. He was also increasingly aware that much of the northeastern United States still clung to its Puritan roots and was actually hostile to Catholicism (many settlers had gone to America to avoid Catholicism in the first place). In February 1968 he won his case against the railroad and received $145,000 in compensation—a great deal of money at that time. This helped Hutton make a decision: he would take his family to the other side of the world, to Australia—a country where he hoped stricter moral values still prevailed.

Hutton Gibson wanted the journey to Australia to be an educational, leisurely tour rather than a direct flight, so the family visited Ireland and Scotland, to teach the children about their family background; England; and Rome, where the family spent much time at the Vatican, the center of their faith. Mel also nearly got lost at Leonardo da Vinci airport.

The family arrived in Melbourne in November 1968 and moved almost immediately to a suburb north of Sydney. Mel was sent to St. Leo's College, a traditionalist Catholic school then run by the Christian Brothers. This was something of an ordeal for him; he was teased mercilessly for his American accent and the Brothers were quite renowned for running a strict regime. In response Mel became something of a rebel, taking up smoking and drinking and engaging in pranks designed to irritate his teachers. Eventually, though, he was rescued from the school by his father (because Hutton did not consider the religious teaching adequate) and sent to Asquith High, a state school. Here Mel was much happier and became effectively "Australianized." He continued to be regarded as something of an entertainer but otherwise did not shine at school. Meanwhile his father was becoming increasingly isolated from the Catholic Church until he eventually broke away completely from the official Church. At home he continued to teach his children a highly conservative, rigid religion.

At school, Mel continued to indulge in behavior typical of many teenagers—drinking beer, smoking, and starting to date girls. Contrary to the reputation he was later to develop as a heartthrob, at first he was apparently shy and gawky. Eventually school came to an end and Mel had to think of a career. During his early teens, due to his father's influence, he had considered entering the priesthood; by the time he left school he no longer felt this calling. Journalism was considered and rejected—perhaps appropriately in view of Mel's later dislike of journalists. But fate took a hand: his sister Sheila, who thought his skill at pranks and pratfalls demonstrated acting talent, filled out an application form and sent it, along with five Australian dollars and a photo, to the National Institute of Dramatic Arts (NIDA) at the University of New South Wales in Sydney.

Mel confronts the camera

Mel Gibson

THE ROAD TO FAME

Mel's approach to his new trade was fairly nonchalant. First of all, he hadn't known that he had applied to drama school; second, he wasn't desperate to be an actor. But at the time of his application to NIDA, he was working in an orange juice bottling plant, and an acting course must have seemed more exciting. Somewhat to his own surprise, Mel was accepted for NIDA, in the face of competition from many who were desperate to become actors. He attributed his success to the fact that he had been forced to resort to subterfuge so often at school that this made him a natural. He had also shown himself a good mimic at school, with a keen ear for accents—after all, he had had to adopt an Australian accent to survive.

NIDA was a rather basic establishment at the time Mel attended, consisting of leaky prefabricated huts at the University of New South Wales. Mel continued to engage in practical jokes and found it hard to take some of the exercises seriously; consequently staff and students at NIDA found his attitude to the course less committed than theirs. Many of the exercises were difficult to perform, such as turning on apparently strong emotions while playing a part under the critical eyes of fellow students and teachers. He also found acting school difficult because he did not share the conviction of the other students that acting was the only thing he wanted to do—it certainly hadn't been his original wish. At the same time he was keenly aware that some of the other "committed" students looked down on him for not having the same outward dedication.

After a year at NIDA Mel moved out of the family home to live with three of his friends. Life got a bit wilder as the four young men threw wild parties, annoyed the neighbors, and chased the girls. Despite this he began to shine at NIDA; not only was he cast as Romeo in the school's production of *Romeo and Juliet*, he also became known as a scene-stealer. Whatever the importance of the role he was playing, his charismatic presence came to dominate the production. His attitude to an acting career was changing and he was beginning to enjoy the work and throw himself into it. When his hair and beard were cut for a forties production, Mel's good looks were at last truly revealed.

In November 1976 it seemed that fame was beckoning, if in a small way. Producer Phil Avalon contacted Mel and his fellow student Steve Bisley and offered them both roles in a low-budget surfing film, *Summer City*, set in the sixties. (*Summer City* had hints of *The Wild One*, *Easy Rider*, and *American Graffiti*, with a plot involving a group of youths arriving in a poky little town where they seduce the local girls and end up facing the guns of the local populace and law enforcers. Fun ends in tragedy, and with it comes the recognition that freedom has its limits.) The total budget was around $100,000 and the actors' fee was $400, the union minimum. It was the sort of operation where everybody had to pitch in and served as a real introduction to the basics of filmmaking for Mel. After the film, Mel returned to NIDA to finish his studies. In later years he has looked back on his time at NIDA with affection despite the early difficulties, and after the release of *Hamlet* he sponsored a scholarship there.

The main benefit of *Summer City*, as far as Mel was concerned, was that his participation attracted the attention of

Bill Shannahan, one of Australia's most prestigious agents. Shannahan got Mel two weeks' work on an Australian soap opera called *The Sullivans*. Through this brief exposure to television, Mel developed an intense almost permanent dislike of the medium (only once more would he work in television). Soaps operate with a minimum amount of rehearsal, both for actors and for scriptwriters; such an arrangement can be profoundly dissatisfying for the serious actor because the emphasis is on getting the series out, not on the quality of the production.

Luckily, Mel's next work was with the South Australian Theatre Company, a touring company for whom he performed in Samuel Beckett's *Waiting for Godot*. The part was physically exhausting and Mel had serious breathing problems due to his heavy smoking. The critics, however, were unaware of this and gave the play excellent reviews. During this tour, while in Adelaide, Mel met Robyn Moore, who would later become his wife. Robyn was a dental assistant who rented a room in the same house, and Mel got to know her over a fairly long period—she already had a boyfriend and Mel had to wait. She is described as being a fairly quiet person but for Mel she was to become a pillar of support in later years. In the meantime, Shannahan was spreading the word about Mel and a new offer came through in September 1977 from Dr. George Miller, a producer-director. Mel couldn't start immediately because he had to finish school and graduate, which he did in October. George Miller held up work on the film until Mel could begin. The movie was *Mad Max*.

Mel Gibson as Mad Max

MAD MAX AND BEYOND

Mel's breakthrough came almost as soon as he had left college. Although nobody expected it Mad Max was to gain worldwide fame (its only poor showing was in the United States). Set in the near future in a postnuclear world, the movie features clearcut villains and heroes, and hardly anybody else. Miller wanted to create a new sort of Western, with the forces of good and evil immediately identifiable. The budget for the film, which was to include a great deal of hair-raising action, was only $250,000—a minuscule amount by Hollywood standards (although Mel's fee was $10,000, a serious sum for a recently graduated actor)—so, like Summer City, making the movie was very much a group activity. Actors helped move equipment and, unlike in Hollywood, there was no hierarchy. The crew and the cast shared a large house in Melbourne (among their number were some real Hell's Angels who played the "Toe Cutters" in the movie). The film's reputation for fairly mindless violence packed the movie houses, and the Australian Film Institute gave it no less than six awards, including best actor for Mel. An important part of its success was that its high-adrenalin automotive action attracted many young male viewers.

The success of Mad Max brought in multiple offers of work and Hollywood agent Ed Limato sought out Mel. It was at the start of a frenetic period of activity for Mel, the first of three films in a year. After *Mad Max*, there was more stage acting in *Oedipus Rex* and *Henry IV* in Adelaide, and another movie project, *Tim*, which was as about as far removed as it could have been from his previous role. Mel played a mentally retarded gardener who develops a relationship with a handsome woman in her mid-forties. She helps to educate him and in so doing revives her own positive attitude toward life. *Tim* helped hone Mel's acting skills: *Mad Max* had not challenged him with dialogue or the demands of playing a particularly multifaceted character. As a perfectionist Mel always wanted to spend more time on each scene of *Tim*, but because he was so quick to pick up director Michael Pate's ideas, much of the film was shot in one take. While not a great international success, *Tim* did earn Mel an Australian Film Institute best actor award in 1979. He was seen as having sensitively developed the role, conveying the innocence of Tim's character rather than his backwardness. The part also demonstrated Mel's ability to embody characters that would appeal to a wider film audience.

After filming was complete, Mel was expected to take part in publicity for the film, and here his reputation for being uncooperative with the press began. Mel's attitude toward acting is that it is a job, and while he is entirely capable of commenting on any aspect of that job, such as his own role, he does not feel it necessarily qualifies him to give his opinion on such broader issues as the direction of the film industry. Mel does not subscribe to the prevalent notion that because stars are so much in the public eye, they are therefore qualified to talk about any issue. And when he does not feel qualified to comment, he does not comment: if he considers a question irrelevant, he won't answer it.

Mel's next film was *Attack Force Z*, a World War II yarn set in the Pacific. Things did not go well. The director initially chosen, Philip Noyce (who later directed *Patriot Games* and *Dead Calm*, among others), fought with the producer over the budget and had to be replaced by Tim Burstall. Most of the cast were unhappy with the change. Apparently Mel and the other Australian actors told Burstall that they simply did not want to do the film with him. The only cast member who did not seem to object to Burstall was American actor John Philip Law, the star of the film; his fee was $50,000 as opposed to the $1,000 a week that Mel and New Zealander Sam Neill received. Law also stayed in a decent hotel while the other accommodations were shabby. Also, at six-foot-five, Law had to adopt some ridiculous poses to make himself appear to be of similar height to Mel. (Mel's height seems to have varied slightly over the years, depending on who you believe, but the general consensus is that he is five-eight or five-nine.) To save money, the film was shot in Taiwan. The completed film did receive good reviews, though it was not released in America. Mel had been unhappy with the whole project, drowning his sorrows in copious amounts of Taiwanese beer during the shoot, and made scathing comments about the movie itself thereafter. After this film, Mel determined not to act in any more low-budget movies.

Roughly six months after the end of shooting, on June 7, 1980, Mel married Robyn Moore in Forestville, New South Wales. The couple honeymooned north of Sydney at a friend's house. The need for money began to press on Mel (*Attack Force Z* had earned him only $6,000), and he accepted a part in the TV series *Punishment*, one of several Australian prison dramas. As with *The Sullivans*, he disliked the process of TV production, where tight schedules and arduous hours allowed no time to develop a character. His necessity to continue with TV work ended, though, when Peter Weir—the director of *Picnic at Hanging Rock*, a film that had done much to alert the world to the renaissance in Australian moviemaking—approached Bill Shannahan to see if Mel could act in his forthcoming film *Gallipoli*.

The Gallipoli campaign, a military disaster, had burned itself into the Australian consciousness, because such a large number of the forces involved were Australians and New Zealanders. It was similar in its impact to the Western Front for the British and French. Essentially it was a rite of passage, both for the nation, and for the innocent young men involved—most of whom had never been abroad, let alone introduced to the horrors of modern warfare. The sacrifice made Australia feel that it was on equal footing with its mother country (Great Britain) and was no longer a colony. The film portrays the story through the eyes of Frank and Archie, two country boys who think they are off to save the world. Their experiences soon disillusion them, though the grim reality of their situation is partly offset by the comradeship that develops between them.

The film was shot under some difficult conditions. The outback at Beltana, where the action begins and the camel racing takes place, was dusty and blisteringly hot. Lake Torrens was bitterly cold. Conditions improved, though, when filming moved into the congenial town of Port Lincoln, where a reconstruction of Anzac Cove had been built on the coast. The final shoot took place in Egypt, since Cairo had been the way station for ANZACs destined for Gallipoli. While Mel was in filming Cairo his first child, Hannah, was born.

Reviews of the film were excellent. It was received rapturously in Australia, where it garnered nine awards from the Australian Film Institute, including another best actor award for Mel. Although some British papers questioned the anti-British sentiments expressed in the film, it also did well in Britain.

Gallipoli was followed up in 1981 by *Mad Max II—The Road Warrior*. In its classic Western plot, a roving law enforcer comes to the rescue of a civilized settlement under attack from savages, distinguished by their ruthless brutality and their eccentric machinery. Mad Max has returned in a somewhat damaged state. Full of spectacular stunts, the picture is solid action and not for the squeamish. The final

HEBRON PUBLIC SCHOOL LIBRARY

Young soldiers Gibson and Lee in Gallipoli

scenes, in which Mel draws off the assailants while the townsfolk head off in another direction, are particularly gripping. *The Road Warrior* eventually grossed more than *Mad Max*, making over $100 million. It faired respectably in the United States, where it earned $24 million. Unlike *Mad Max,* which had mainly been popular with young men, *The Road Warrior* also found a female audience, eager to see the attractive leading man.

Mel often expressed his wish to get away from being typecast as a law enforcer (Mad Max was actually a policeman) or as a soldier. His next project was to satisfy this wish. After the success of *Gallipoli*, Peter Weir signed Mel on for another project, *The Year of Living Dangerously.* Set in Indonesia in 1965, in a period of great political turmoil, the movie starred Mel as an Australian journalist who has an affair with a British diplomat, played by Sigourney Weaver. (Because Sigourney Weaver is so tall, Mel had to have his shoes built up to match her height.) Mel has always said that he plays a part from outside, and this was his first encounter with different American schools of acting, a process he found educative, though he has never become a method actor (whereby actors try to become the character they are playing, by behaving like that character all the time).

Filming was difficult. Most of the location work was done in the Philippines, and the cast was subject to death threats from local fanatics who thought the movie would be disrespectful to their religion. Because of these problems, toward the end of the shoot some scenes were shot in Australia; this suited Mel since his wife gave birth to twins on June 2, 1982, and he was able to be present this time. Though well crafted, the film did not seem to catch the imagination of audiences and was not the success it might have been. However, it did take Mel to Cannes for a screening at the annual film festival in May 1983, where he was compared to other male heroes—John Wayne from the older generation, and

Madder still, Mad Max II

Harrison Ford and Tom Selleck from the new.

After *Living Dangerously* Mel turned down several lucrative film roles arranged for him by Ed Limato in Hollywood, choosing instead to take the part of Biff in Arthur Miller's *Death of a Salesman*, which played in Sydney for two months in the autumn of 1982. Mel has declared that stage acting is preferable to film work as a means of honing one's acting skills, since a genuine audience response is possible with stage work, whereas in films the only real audience present to respond to an actor's performance is the director. But, despite Mel's preference for Australia, Hollywood still beckoned, and Ed Limato got Mel a role in *The Running Man*, though he withdrew before production to take the role of Mr. Christian in *The Bounty*.

The Bounty was shot on Mooréa, an island off Tahiti. Though it may sound like the perfect holiday destination, working continually in such a place for four months can become quite claustrophobic, with little in the way of entertainment. All in all, the shooting of the film was not a particularly good period for Mel, and harsh words were said about his behavior. Later, when the film was released, the reviews were equally critical. Remakes of classics are highly risky: not only are they criticized in their own right, but also in relation to the originals. *The Mutiny on the Bounty* has received several film treatments over the years, including the classic 1962 Trevor Howard/Marlon Brando version, and this one did not fare well by comparison.

Mel is decorated in The Bounty

An argument with Danny Glover in Lethal Weapon

AMERICAN DEBUT

After *The Bounty*, Mel went on to play his first screen role as an American, and an American with a Tennessee accent at that. Director Mark Rydell had serious doubts about casting Mel in the part of a country farmer in *The River*, because he assumed Mel would have an Australian accent. But Mel's ability to mimic convinced him and Mel got the lead role, playing opposite Sissy Spacek. The film was shot in eastern Tennessee and Robyn and the family came to stay nearby. It received moderate acclaim, most of it for Sissy Spacek, who received an Oscar nomination. Mel's next role was in a film called *Mrs. Soffel*, where he played opposite Diane Keaton; he was a prisoner, and she the warder's wife who falls in love with him. The shooting conditions, in Canada and Pittsburgh, were miserable, since much of the time was spent hanging round in the freezing cold. Mel's drinking problem also received prominence—on April 25, 1984, he was picked up for drunk driving, for which he received a three-month suspension and a $300 fine. The reaction to the film itself was pretty mixed; Diane Keaton and Mel Gibson did not seem to have the right chemistry.

Meanwhile, the ghost of *Mad Max* had reappeared. Hollywood was now interested, given the success of his previous two incarnations, and Warner Bros. was prepared to make a big-budget sequel. *Mad Max—Beyond Thunderdome* was shot right in the middle of Australia, at Coober Pedy, five hundred miles northwest of Adelaide, where the temperatures were so high that several members of the crew were struck down by heat exhaustion. Having taken only a three-month break, Mel was tired from the films he had recently completed, and apparently took to the bottle in a big way. Reputedly he was knocking back five bottles of beer before starting work, and drinking more through all the rest periods. Not only did he miss his family, but his previous three films had made no real impact and consequently he seemed to be facing the end of any future he might have in Hollywood. He needn't have worried. *Beyond Thunderdome* was a great success, making $40 million in the United States alone.

Afterward Mel decided to take a proper break. Like his father had been, Mel is interested in farming, and he bought a farm in northern Victoria, which he began to work. He also wanted to reestablish his links with his family after spending so much time away from them. Together with Australian producer Pat Lovell, he formed a production company—Lovell Gibson—with the idea of developing film projects in Australia. Unfortunately things did not quite work out as planned, since Hollywood producer Jerry Weintraub suggested a link-up that would give him first refusal on any projects Lovell Gibson came up with. There was also one condition: Mel would have to star.

Soon after the company's foundation, Mel headed off to Hollywood to make *Lethal Weapon*, taking his family with him. Set in the genre at which Mel excelled, *Lethal Weapon* used the formula of two men—Marty Riggs and Roger Murtaugh (played by Danny Glover)—one active and aggressive, one older and wiser, who are thrown together by their work and don't initially respect each other's qualities, but later come to do so. The movie is full of violence and has no romantic interest. Mel appreciated the character of Marty, a suicidal loner, a Vietnam veteran whose wife had died and whose world has fallen apart. Being a very private person, he could empathize with the part. As method actor, Danny Glover took a completely different approach than Mel's, but nonetheless the two leads got along reasonably well. Their different approaches mirrored the differences between the characters they played—one more impulsive, one more reflective, thereby achieving the intention of the director, Richard Donner (of *Superman* fame). Donner had been worried that Mel would cause problems during production, but Mel was highly professional. He had benefited from his break, and from having Robyn there with him, and he managed to stay away from alcohol. But when Robyn left shortly after the film's completion and Mel stayed on in his Santa Monica apartment, he soon started to drink again.

During the Cannes Festival of 1987, which he attended to promote *Lethal Weapon*, Mel had to engage in typical "star" activities such as setting his palm in concrete. He was also the focus of attention of several women, some of whom were rich and powerful. He apparently found the glitz and glamour all too much; he retired from his hotel to a yacht Jerry Weintraub had chartered, and gave himself over to the bottle. Eventually he had had enough and asked Pat Lovell to arrange for his immediate return to Sydney and the family.

Lethal Weapon, in its three installments, did amazingly well at the box office, peaking at $300 million for *Lethal Weapon 3* in 1992. Critically the reaction was mixed. The level of violence was extremely high and the movies provoked much debate about whether celluloid violence was imitated on the street. The argument still occurs, as effects get ever more realistic and gory. Yet the public continues to display an appetite for violence, as evidenced by the success of films such as the *Terminator* series or *Robocop*. The question of whether it is better to portray violence in a fantasy world or in ugly reality as in *Lethal Weapon* is one of the issues at the heart of the debate.

Mel's partnership with Pat Lovell came to an end in January 1989, when Mel formed a production company in Los Angeles. Lovell was eventually paid $1 for her share in the folded company. Ed Limato's strenuous efforts to keep Mel in the United States seemed to be paying off. In 1990 Bill Shannahan died; he had been a mentor as well as an agent for Mel and had made an effort to keep Mel working in Australia. During the late eighties, though, Mel's particular wish was to work in a comedy film, partly because Paul Hogan was so successful in *Crocodile Dundee*, but also because Mel didn't wish to be stereotyped and wanted to extend his acting range. Such a project never came up.

At the time when *Lethal Weapon* was released, Mel had his first flirtation with politics. While not eligible to vote in Australia because of his American passport, he clearly feels that it is his adopted land and he takes an interest in issues there. The person he chose to support in 1987 was Robert Taylor, a fundamentalist conservative. People turned up to the rallies, presumably to see Mel rather than listen to Taylor's extreme pronouncements. Liberal Australia, as represented by the quality press, found Mel's association unusual. Mel was perhaps taking after his father, the man for whom the Roman Catholic Church was too liberal. Two years later he was to support Barry Tattersall, another independent candidate during the federal elections, and express views such as support of capital punishment, loathing of high taxation and government intervention, and disapproval over the apparent moral decline of the West.

After the success of *Lethal Weapon*, the offers flooded in for work. Mel was even offered a role in the long-running soap *Dallas*, at the instigation of Victoria Principal. (Of course, she had no idea of Mel's deep-seated aversion to TV work, whatever the money.) Mel bought a house in Malibu after the second *Lethal Weapon* film, since Los Angeles was becoming his base and his loyalties were shifting from Australia to the United States. There has been some slight resentment in Australia at this shift; naturally, Australians like to regard Mel as one of their own because he had become so Australianized and began his successful career there. But Mel has never given up his American passport and the United States is his native country. And though Mel had resisted the lures of Tinseltown, Hollywood is renowned for getting ahold of people and keeping them there, at least as long as they are successful. Also, as the children grow older, Robyn has insisted that they need to be educated in one place, which currently means staying in Los Angeles.

The next project Mel accepted was *Tequila Sunrise,* in which he played an erstwhile drug dealer, despite having refused such a role in earlier days when he stated that it was morally offensive to him. His character, Dale McKussic, has effectively reformed by the start of the film, and the story revolves around his confrontation with an old school friend who is in the drug squad, including rivalry for the attentions of the character played by Michelle Pfeiffer. The film received mixed reviews, partly because reviewers found it hard to believe that an ex–drug dealer was a suitable hero for a romantic comedy. Its box office receipts in the United States were less than half those of *Lethal Weapon.*

Kurt Russell played opposite Mel in *Tequila Sunrise*, and the two became good friends. Russell's partner is Goldie Hawn, who effectively started her career in the sixties television comedy series *Rowan and Martin's Laugh-in.* A new project was put together for Mel and Goldie; entitled *Bird on a Wire,* it was a fairly brainless chase movie but it did quite well, earning the same as *Lethal Weapon* in the States. When *Bird on a Wire* was over, Mel headed back to Australia for some well-deserved rest on his farm.

Mel interprets Hamlet

THE ESTABLISHED STAR

In 1987 some of the British tabloids began to spread rumors that Mel was dating Cassandra Kirton, an English girl he had met in Los Angeles. Another story, from late 1986, links him with Miranda Brewin, another English girl he had met in Sydney. Mel threatened legal action and the papers retracted. Both girls denied that anything untoward had happened. These stories were followed up by articles in 1993 in an American tabloid, the *Globe*, which carried pictures of Mel allegedly fooling around with some women in a bar in Modesto, California. Mel's lawyers threatened the *Globe* with a lawsuit, though this never materialized. As a result of the latter incident Mel decided that his drinking was getting out of hand, and that the publication of these sort of stories did his marriage no good. In the middle of 1991 he had joined Alcoholics Anonymous, because Ed Limato and Robyn were both very concerned about the effect alcohol might have on his career. Furthermore, the mood around the country, and in Hollywood in particular, was growing hostile to alcohol. After the Modesto escapade, he attended more AA meetings while continuing to fulfill his obligations on the set.

Shooting for Mel's next major project, *Air America*, began in early 1990. The film was based on the activities of the CIA in running an airline into Laos during the Vietnam War. Filming was done near the Golden Triangle,

31

the notorious drug-growing area in the north of Thailand and Laos. Robyn and the family came to join Mel for a while, which helped keep him calm during the making of the film. The cast and crew were working in isolated jungle conditions, with all the attendant discomforts—mosquitoes, torrential rain, and very basic accommodations. After a while, Robyn returned to Australia to give birth to their sixth child. Mel reverted to his usual pattern of heavy drinking, arguing, and waking up bad-tempered, often feeling guilty about his behavior the night before. This ended after Robyn had given birth to Milo and returned a few weeks later to Thailand. Mel was relieved when shooting was over and he could return to Australia to be with his family and newborn son.

The net result of all this discomfort was not a success. The producers wanted a more cheerful ending after seeing the final product, as if failing to recognize that *Air America* dealt with a sordid period in the country's foreign policy, whatever the individual bravery and morality of the pilots involved. A different ending was tacked on, with Mel doing the final scenes in Shepperton Studios. Many veterans of the real Air America complained vociferously, believing that the film trivialized their efforts.

After the poor showing of *Air America*, Mel's next project was as different as it could possibly be. Twenty years earlier Franco Zeffirelli had made a successful film version of *Romeo and Juliet*, starring two virtual unknowns, Leonard Whiting and Olivia Hussey. This had been an unexpected runaway success. Since then, he had made *The Taming of the Shrew*, with Richard Burton and Elizabeth Taylor, which had done moderately well. Zeffirelli was renowned for a somewhat lavish approach to Shakespeare that did not always fare well with the critics, even if audiences enjoyed it. Zeffirelli persuaded Mel to star in a movie version of *Hamlet*. The budget for the film was substantial—$15 million, most of which reputedly came from Warner Bros., which was

With Goldie Hawn in Bird on a Wire

anxious to sign Mel to a long-term contract. News of Mel's reincarnation as the Prince of Denmark was greeted with virtual incredulity. Not all of his roles had been rich in dialogue, and here he was, about to embark on a project that was 99 percent dialogue, 1 percent action. Furthermore, the cast included some highly respected names—Glenn Close, Alan Bates, Ian Holm, and Helena Bonham-Carter.

Mel became utterly absorbed in the part. Many of those who laughed at him were unaware that he had already been in several well-received serious stage productions. Indeed, if it weren't for the money to be made in films, the stage would have had more of his time. But this was his first venture into film for the type of audience that attends the serious theater. He was aware of the possible reaction of such an audience and it added to the tension he felt at playing the part. But despite any initial reservations they may have had, his fellow actors came to respect Mel's performance. He was glad, though, when shooting came to an end.

Unusually, Mel threw himself enthusiastically into promoting the film, entirely changing his demeanor to the press. The only difficult part for him was that his mother died in December 1990, just before the U.S. release, and he was disappointed that she would never see him in the sort of role to which he had always aspired. Nevertheless, he continued with the film's promotion after returning to Australia for her funeral.

The period before *Hamlet*'s review by the press must have been an anxious one for Mel, but he needn't have worried. The reviews in the United States were almost entirely favorable and most Australian critics applauded it. Reservations were strongest in the United Kingdom, where it was felt that Mel's interpretation was a little wooden, solid but missing the nuances. Whatever one's view, the movie did help to popularize Shakespeare. He didn't receive an Oscar for the part but he was given a Will Award by the Shakespeare Theatre in Washington, D.C. After *Hamlet* Mel

Taken prisoner in Laos in Air America

headed off to his farm in Australia for a long, well-earned rest.

In the meantime, Hollywood had moved on. Kevin Costner's *Dances with Wolves* had become a phenomenal success, and Mel wanted to find a project that would keep him in the same league. (The two had met several years earlier at Cannes, when Mel's pulling power with producers was far ahead of Costner's; Mel had also been offered the lead in *Robin Hood: Prince of Thieves*, which Costner had taken.) Although Mel's next work was on *Lethal Weapon 3*, which grossed over $160 million in the United States, he was seeking something new to broaden his acting range. The project Mel came up with was *Forever Young,* whose story concerns a hero cryogenically preserved for fifty years who emerges to face a strange world. The film was lightweight but nonetheless did well enough at the box office to prove Mel's drawing power.

In February 1991 Warner Bros. signed a $42 million deal with Mel for a four-film partnership. Mel would also get royalties and his production company, Icon Productions, would produce the films. Mel also wanted to direct, and got his chance in *The Man without a Face*, for which he both directed and acted and which was well reviewed after its release in 1993. He played a burn victim who befriends a small boy, until small-minded townsfolk drive him off. Many adult actors find it difficult to work with children, but Mel does not consider this a problem; he enjoys working with them and has a much more natural manner with them than most other actors. Over the years he has also been involved in charitable work for children.

In his next film, Mel achieved a long-held desire to act in a Western, a genre that was undergoing something of a renaissance with Clint Eastwood's *Unforgiven* and Costner's *Dances with Wolves* both doing fantastically well. The subject Mel chose was *Maverick*, which had been a TV series in the sixties. To script the project he hired William Goldman (the screenwriter responsible for *Butch Cassidy and the Sundance*

With James Garner and Jodie Foster in Maverick

Kid, among many other films), and he acquired the services of Richard Donner of the *Lethal Weapon* series to direct. The story revolves round the attempts of gambler Brett Maverick and Annabelle Bransford (played by Jodie Foster) to raise money to enter a gambling competition. James Garner, the original star of the TV series, plays Zane Cooper, who attempts to thwart Maverick's efforts and steal his girlfriend. It was released in the summer of 1994.

Then came *Braveheart,* the story of the struggle of the Scots, led by Sir William Wallace, against the invading English. Mel may have seen it as his reply to *Robin Hood: Prince of Thieves*, basing the film on a historical rather than a legendary figure. The film took some slight liberties with history, such as in the flirtation between Wallace and Princess Isabelle, or the portrayal of Wallace as a humble peasant rather than the son of a landowner. Also Wallace was in reality involved in only two major battles, for Stirling (a victory in 1297) and for Falkirk (a defeat in 1298), and was captured and executed in 1305, two years before Edward I's death. But Wallace is more than just history, he is the stuff of legend, and he fought for independence against the English, something with which Mel, with his Irish ancestry, sympathized. The scriptwriter was Randall Wallace, who had developed an interest in his namesake on a visit to Edinburgh, and his screenplay was brought to Mel's attention by coproducer Alan Ladd, Jr.

Braveheart was the first film over which Mel had overall artistic control: he served as producer and director as well leading actor. Shooting was carried out on location in Scotland and Ireland, with sets incorporating genuine medieval buildings such as Trim Castle in Ireland. The realistic goriness of the battle scenes—which employed seventeen hundred Irish Army reserves as extras—was enough to ensure the film a restricted-viewing rating in several countries. Shooting concluded at the end of October 1994, and the film was released in autumn 1995.

As Wallace in the Academy Award–winning Braveheart

Braveheart was put up by Paramount for a whole clutch of Oscar nominations—Best Picture, Best Director for Mel, Best Screenplay, Best Cinematography, Best Costume Design, Best Sound, Best Film Editing, Best Sound Effects Editing, Best Makeup, and Best Music and Original Dramatic Score. In the end it won five Oscars, including Best Picture, and Mel was awarded the highly coveted award for Best Director. Appropriately, he accepted the awards wearing a tartan waistcoat.

In 1996 Mel appeared in the highly acclaimed film *Ransom*. He had a brief, uncredited cameo as a tattooed rock fan in 1997's *Father's Day*. Given the increasing diversity of Mel's output, he appears to have many choices about what avenues he will pursue—perhaps more comedy, more serious drama, or more historical epics. What is clear is that he has a hankering for roles other than those to which he owes most of his fame—Mad Max and Marty Riggs. Mel has arrived on the Hollywood scene as a fully fledged all-around actor whose work, as he matures, puts him up with the movie greats.

Mel and Sigourney Weaver in The Year of Living Dangerously

Gibson and young friend Nick Stahl in The Man without a Face

FILMOGRAPHY

The year refers to the first release date of the film.

1978   *Summer City*
1979   *Mad Max*
1979   *Tim*
1981   *Gallipoli*
1981   *Mad Max II—The Road Warrior*
1981   *Attack Force Z*
1982   *The Year of Living Dangerously*
1984   *The Bounty*
1984   *The River*
1984   *Mrs. Soffel*
1985   *Mad Max III—Beyond Thunderdome*
1987   *Lethal Weapon*
1988   *Tequila Sunrise*
1989   *Lethal Weapon 2*
1990   *Bird on a Wire*
1990   *Air America*
1991   *Hamlet*
1992   *Lethal Weapon 3*
1992   *Forever Young*
1993   *The Man Without a Face*
1994   *Maverick*
1995   *Braveheart*
1996   *Ransom*
1997   *Conspiracy Theory*

With Isabel Lasser in Forever Young

ACKNOWLEDGMENTS

Aquarius

Associated R&R Films/Paramount (courtesy Kobal)

Icon Productions (courtesy Kobal)

Kobal Collection

Mad Max (courtesy Kobal)

MGM/UA (courtesy Kobal)

Orion (courtesy Kobal)

Paramount (courtesy Kobal)

TriStar (courtesy Kobal)

Universal (courtesy Kobal)

Warner Bros. (courtesy Kobal)

INDEX

INDEX